PAPERWHITE USER Guide

HOW TO USE *KINDLE PAPERWHITE*

By Emery H. Maxwell

Table of Contents

Welcome

Welcome to the *PAPERWHITE USER GUIDE*. This manual is intended to help you understand and manage the different features of the *PAPERWHITE* device.

Starting with the basics, this book is intended to help you understand what the *KINDLE PAPERWHITE* device can do and how to do it.

Using the tablet might be simple, but not everything about it is entirely intuitive. In fact, trying to figure it out by yourself can be overwhelming, especially if you have never owned a digital reader before.

This is where a guide can be very useful.

This guide is intended to help improve your understanding and usage of the *KINDLE PAPERWHITE* tablet, including how to maximize its features.

It will cover:

• How to set up the device

• How to navigate the device

• How to navigate books

• How to access and use the onscreen keyboard

• How to get more out of your reading experience

• How to add multiple household member accounts to your *Kindle*

• How to borrow books from the public library online (Currently only available in the U.S.)

• How to manage your content

• Troubleshooting

• . . . and more.

It's time to get started.

Getting Started

The following chapters will help you understand the *KINDLE PAPERWHITE*. They will go over specifications, basic hardware, status indicators, and setting up the device.

Specifications

- **Included in the box:** *Kindle* device, USB 2.0 charging cable, and Quick Start Guide

- **Size:** 6.7" x 4.6" x 0.36"

- **Weight:** WI-FI: 7.2 oz. WI-FI + Free Cellular Connectivity: 7.6 oz

- **Screen Size:** 6" glare-free

- **Resolution:** 300 PPI

- **Storage:** 4 GB

- **Connectivity:** WI-FI or WI-FI + Free Cellular Connectivity

- **WI-FI Connectivity:** Supports public and private WI-FI networks that use the 802.11b, 802.11g, or 802.11n standard with support for WPA, WPA2, and WEP security using password authentication or WI-FI Protection Setup

- **Battery Life:** Up to six weeks, but will vary based on wireless and light usage

- **Charge Time:** Fully charges in approximately 4 hours from a computer through USB cable

- **System Requirements:** None; fully wireless and does not require a computer to download content

- **Cloud Storage:** Cloud storage is free for all *Amazon* content

- **Accessibility Features:** *Voice-View* screen reader, activated by the *Kindle* Audio Adapter

- **Supported Content Formats:** HTML, DOC, DOCX, JPEG, GIF, PNG, BMP through conversion; AZW3, AZW, TXT, PDF, unprotected MOBI, PRC

- **Audible:** No

- **Built-in Light:** Yes - 4 LED

- **Page Turns:** Touchscreen

- **Waterproof:** No

- **Storage Temperature:** 14°F to 113°F (-10°C to 45°C)

Basic Hardware

• **Power Button:** Located on the bottom edge of the device. Pressing this button will power on the device. To turn off the screen, press and hold this button for approximately 7 seconds until the Power dialog box displays, then tap *Screen Off.*

Sleep mode

The device goes into sleep mode automatically after a few minutes of inactivity. The static screen saver that becomes displayed in sleep mode does not use battery power.

The *Kindle* can be placed in sleep mode by pressing and releasing the power button. To wake up the device, press and release the power button.

Depending on the device, it might be possible to adjust the sleep mode timeout by going to *Settings > More > Display > Screen Timeout.*

To disable sleep mode, go to the search bar and enter the command ~DS. If this is done successfully, you will not be able to lock the *Kindle* device until the next restart. Restarting the device should restore the screen saver lock and bring it back to normal.

Restarting

If the device becomes unresponsive, a forced restart might be necessary. To restart the *Kindle*, press and hold the power button for approximately 7 seconds until the dialog box appears, then tap *Restart*. If the device becomes so unresponsive that it does not display the dialog box, press and hold the power button for approximately 40 seconds or until the LED light ceases blinking.

Micro-USB: This slot is located next to the power button. The supplied USB cable can be connected to the *Kindle* device via a computer for transferring files and charging the battery. Charging the *Kindle* device from a power outlet requires a compatible AC adapter (sold separately) for the USB cable.

Touchscreen interface: The touchscreen interface allows the user to perform various tasks with a tap or swipe of a fingertip. Items can be opened by tapping them. To illustrate, a book can be opened by tapping the book cover. Additionally, a button can be tapped to perform the action of that button.

Status Indicators

T he status indicators are located at the top of the main screen (Home screen). They are there to keep you informed of battery status, activity status, and more. There is also a parental controls indicator if you choose to enable it.

Tip: If you are reading a book or document, the indicators can still be viewed by tapping the top of the screen.

• **Battery status indicator:** reveals the various stages of the battery as it discharges. It will display a lighting bolt on the battery icon while the *Kindle* device is charging.

• **Activity indicator:** can be seen in the top left corner of the *Kindle* screen while it is loading a web page, downloading content, connecting to a network, opening a large PDF file, or checking for new items.

• **Parental Controls indicator:** can be seen when Parental Controls are enabled.

• **Voice-View indicators:** speaker icon that lets you know *screen reader* is powered on.

• **WI-FI icon:** Lets you know that the device is connected to *WHISPERNET* using WI-FI.

• **3G icon:** Lets you know that the device is connected to *WHISPERNET* using a 3G cellular network.

• **Airplane icon:** Lets you know that the device is in Airplane Mode and you do not have wireless connectivity.

Setting Up The Device

1.) Make sure the device is charged, then power it on. Wait for it to load. You will eventually be greeted by the *Welcome* screen.

2.) Select a language to use.

3.) When you get to the *Connect to WI-FI* screen, select your WI-FI network. If this is your first time using the device, you will probably need to enter a password first. Then tap **Connect**.

If you do not know your WI-FI password or which network you use, refer to your Internet Service Provider or router manufacturer.

4.) Now it's time to register the device. Start by signing in to your account. If you don't have an account already, go to **Create a new account** and follow the prompts. Select **Register** to complete the registration process.

Tip: To register a *Kindle* device that has already been registered in the past, look at the toolbar and go to **Quick Actions**. From there, select **All Settings**. Go to the **My Account** section, then **REGISTER/DEREGISTER DEVICE**.

While setting up the *Kindle* device, you will also have the option to link your *Kindle* device to your social networking accounts.

After the device is set up, there are some additional tasks you might like to do, such as changing the device's name or adjusting the text.

How to Change The Device's Name

1.) Go to the menu (icon with three dots).

2.) Go to **Settings**.

3.) Select **Device Options**.

4.) Select **Personalize your *Kindle*.**

5.) Go to **Device Name**.

How to Adjust The Text

1.) Go to **Settings**.

2.) Look under **Reading Options**.

3.) Activate/deactivate the **Partial Page Refresh** feature.

There are pros and cons to consider when activating or deactivating this feature. While partial page refresh is smoother and faster, it can lead to afterimage effects. Full page refresh will flash with every page turn, but it also darkens and sharpens the text.

Network Connectivity

M aterial, including books and magazines, are delivered to your *Kindle* through its built-in network connectivity. The *Kindle* e-reader is capable of connecting to your WI-FI network at your home, as well as networks at libraries, airports, etc.

How to Connect Manually

1.) Select the **Quick Actions** icon on the toolbar, then go to **Settings**.

2.) Tap **Wireless**.

3.) A list of WI-FI networks should be displayed. If your network doesn't appear in the list, tap the **RESCAN** button to try again.

4.) Select your network and enter the password if prompted. The password should be located on the router.

5.) Tap **Connect**.

How to Connect Via WPS

1.) Select the **Quick Actions** icon on the toolbar, then go to **Settings**.

2.) Tap **Wireless**.

3.) A list of WI-FI networks should be displayed. If your network doesn't appear in the list, tap the **RESCAN** button to try again.

4.) Select your network.

5.) Press the **WPS** button on your router.

6.) Enter the network password if prompted.

7.) Tap the **WPS** button.

Note: The *Kindle* device does not support peer-to-peer WI-FI networks.

Saved WI-FI Password Management

Saving your WI-FI password to *Amazon* is an option when connecting to a network. Choosing to save your password can help *Amazon* configure your compatible devices, which will eliminate the need to reenter the password for each device.

Change your password

1.) Repeat the WI-FI setup process.

2.) Connect to your WI-FI network.

Delete a saved WI-FI password

1.) Tap **Quick Actions** on the toolbar.

2.) Tap **All Settings**.

3.) Select **Device Options**.

4.) Select **Advanced Options**.

5.) Select **Delete Saved WI-FI Passwords**.

Turn off Wireless and enter Airplane Mode

1.) Tap **Quick Actions (menu)** on the toolbar.

2.) Select **Airplane Mode**.

How to Navigate

This section will go over the fundamentals of *PAPERWHITE* navigation.

There is a main toolbar, which allows the user to access the main features of the device; a reading toolbar that is specifically used for the reading feature; and a periodical toolbar that can be used while reading periodicals.

Each toolbar has its own set of options.

Main Toolbar

The toolbar at the top of the screen contains various icons that allow you to perform a variety of tasks, including navigation.

When you're reading a book or performing some other task, the toolbar often disappears from the screen. If you don't see the toolbar, simply tap the top of the screen to make it appear.

Description of icons on the main toolbar

Home (House icon): Tapping this icon will bring you to the Home screen.

If you are in a store, game, or book, and you'd like to get back to the Home screen, tapping the top of the screen will bring up the toolbar. From there, select the *Home* icon to go back to the Home screen.

Back arrow: Tapping this icon will bring you back to the previous screen page you were on.

Quick Actions: Tapping this icon will give you access to screen light controls, Airplane Mode, Sync My *Kindle*, and *All Settings*.

Screen Light: Tap this icon to access the lighting feature. Simply tap anywhere on the slider—or drag your finger along the slider—to adjust the screen brightness. The plus and minus signs can also be tapped (or tapped and held) for screen brightness adjustment.

***Kindle* Store (Shopping Cart icon):** Select this icon to go to the *Kindle* Store. The device must be connected to the internet to use this option.

Search: Brings up the search field. Tap the X on the right side of the search bar to close it.

Menu: Select this icon to display a list of options.

To keep the options relevant, the menu will change based on what the user is doing.

To illustrate, tapping the menu option while reading a book will bring up options referring to the book, such as *About the Author, Portrait or Landscape mode, About This Book,* etc. Selecting the menu option on the home screen might include *Shop Kindle Store, View Special Offers, Settings,* etc.

Reading Toolbar

Tap the top of the screen to display the reading toolbar.

Display Settings (Text): Select this tab to begin changing font size, line spacing, margins, typeface, and publisher font.

Go To: This is how the user can navigate content. This tab displays the contents of the book, including chapter titles. The options displayed will differ depending on the type of content the user is reading.

X-Ray: Allows the user to view notable clips and images from a book via an organized timeline. This feature will scan the book, and then a dialog box will appear. Tap one of the links in the dialog box to view the results.

When you are reading the *X-Ray* enabled book, tap the top of the screen to display the reading toolbar. From there, tap the *X-Ray* button.

If you don't see the *X-Ray* option displayed, it may mean the option is not available for that particular book.

To discover whether or not a *Kindle* book has the *X-Ray* feature before you purchase it, check the description on the book's sales page.

Share: Select this tab to share your thoughts with friends on social networks.

Bookmarks: Select this tab to add or delete a bookmark and view previously added bookmarks.

Periodical Toolbar

Tap the top of the screen to display the periodical toolbar.

Periodical Home: Displays highlights of the issue you are reading.

Sections and Articles: Select this tab to go to the list of sections and articles in a magazine or newspaper. **Note:** This option is not available in blogs.

If you are reading a periodical and happen to be on the article page, another toolbar can be displayed, featuring more options.

The options include:

Display Settings (Text): Use this to adjust font size, typeface, line spacing, and margins.

Clip This Article: Select this tab to "clip" a periodical article to the *My Clippings* file, which stores your notes, highlights, bookmarks, and clipped articles. The *My Clippings* file is located on the Home screen.

Depending on which version you are using, your *Kindle* might have a tab called **Export Notes.** It is a feature that allows you to send PDF and spreadsheet documents to your e-mail.

Voice-View Screen Reader

When enabled, the *Voice-View Screen Reader* allows you to navigate the *Kindle* device using gestures. It speaks to you, providing voice guidance when you interact with items on the screen. It also enables you to listen to books.

Voice-View is activated by the *Kindle Audio Adapter* when it's plugged in to the Micro-USB port on the *Kindle* device.

To use the *Kindle* with an audio interface, simply plug your headphones or speakers into the audio jack on the *Kindle Audio Adapter*.

When *Voice-View* is enabled for the first time, a tutorial will be presented.

Manage *Voice-View screen reader settings*

1.) Tap **Quick Actions** on the toolbar.

2.) Select **All Settings**.

3.) Tap **Accessibility**.

How to Access and Use the Onscreen Keyboard

The onscreen keyboard can be accessed by tapping within the search field or by starting other actions that require you to type in information. Simply tap the search field, and the onscreen keyboard should appear at the bottom of the screen.

To bring up the search field, tap the "search" icon on the toolbar.

As you type, the auto-suggest feature will begin to take over. At this point, you can either finish typing in the word and select the "search" button to search for it, or you can select (tap) the word that already appears in the search field.

Using the Keyboard

Enter numbers or symbols: Tap the *123!?* key.

Return to regular keyboard: Tap the *ABC* key.

Enter uppercase letter mode: Tap the *Shift* (arrow pointed upward) key twice.

Exit uppercase letter mode: Tap the *Shift* (arrow pointed upward) key once.

Enter Diacritics and special characters: Press and hold the key for the base letter.

Selecting a keyboard for a different language

1.) Tap the **Menu** button.

2.) Select **Settings**.

3.) Select **Device Options, Language and Dictionaries**.

4.) Select **Keyboards**.

Note: When you have selected multiple languages, a "globe key" (key with a globe icon on it) will be added to the keyboard. Simply tap the globe key to select a different keyboard.

The *Kindle* Store

*K*indle books, singles, newspapers, magazines, and blogs are offered on *Amazon's Kindle* store.

Certain menus will allow you to access the *Kindle* store directly. Otherwise, simply tap the screen to make the toolbar appear. From there, select the Shopping Cart icon.

Maneuver the store by swiping the screen in an upward/downward/side-to-side motion. Select an area of interest by tapping the icon on the screen.

There are multiple ways to search for a title.

Searching for a title

• Search for a title in the search field

• Browse by category

• View the list of personalized recommendations

• Browse the list of best sellers

Making a purchase

Payments/purchases are made through the *1-Click* method, and the item will be delivered directly to your *Kindle*.

There will be multiple tabs on the right side of the detail page's screen. To buy the item, select the **Buy now with 1-Click** tab. If you have a *Kindle Unlimited* membership, you can select the **Read for Free** tab if the book is *Kindle Unlimited* eligible. You will also have the option to receive a free sample on your device or give the book to someone else as a gift. Simply select the appropriate tabs to do so.

Books are downloaded to your *Kindle* immediately (usually in less than one minute), and the download progress will be displayed below the book's cover or title on the Home screen.

Newspapers, magazines and blogs will be delivered to your device as soon as they are published. If your device happens to be in *Airplane Mode* when a new issue becomes available, it will be sent to your device the next time you connect.

How to Borrow Books from The Public Library Online (Currently only available in the U.S.)

Public libraries (over eleven-thousand of them) have digital books available to borrow, although this feature is currently only available in the U.S.

Public library *Kindle* books include features, such as, notes and highlights.

Even after after the library book expires, you will still have access to all of your annotations and bookmarks if you choose to borrow it again or purchase it from the *Kindle* store.

1.) Go to your local public library's web site to see if they carry *Kindle* books. You can also discover whether or not your library branch carries *Kindle* books by visiting the *Amazon Overdrive* website.

2.) Sign in by typing in your library card number and/or pass code. Your pass code can be obtained by visiting your local library.

3.) Go to the EBOOK section of the web site. Different libraries across the country will have different layouts, but if you need assistance, call or visit your local library and ask them for help.

4.) Type a title into the search bar or browse for books.

5.) Click the cover of the title you would like to borrow.

6.) Check out the *Kindle* book.

7.) Click on "Get for *Kindle*," then sign in to your *Amazon* account to have the book sent to your *Kindle* device.

8.) Connect the *Kindle* device to WI-FI (not 3G) and download the title from the **Archived Items** or **Cloud**. Library books cannot be delivered through the *Kindle* device's 3G connection.

If your *Kindle* does not receive the book, try syncing your device manually.

How to Return Books to The Public Library Online

1.) Sign in to your *Amazon* account and go to the **Manage Your Content and Devices** section.

2.) Under **Your Content**, select the **Actions** tab next to the book you'd like to return.

3.) Select **Return This Book**.

4.) Select **Yes** in the pop-up window.

The length of time given to borrow a book will vary from library to library, but as a reminder, *Amazon* will send you an email three days before the book is due and another email when the loan period is over.

Note: Due to certain restrictions, some titles may not be delivered through the wireless connection and may require USB transfer from your computer to your device. Additionally, restricted like these also may not be accessed on *Kindle* reading apps.

How to Navigate a Book

Navigating a book can be accomplished by using *Kindle Page Flip* or the *Go To* button.

Kindle Page Flip will allow you to preview other pages in a book without having to leave the current page. This can be useful when you'd like to navigate the book without losing your place.

Navigating with *Kindle Page Flip*

1.) Swipe upward from the bottom of the screen. This will bring up the *Page Flip* toolbar.

2.) Press and hold the circle, then drag it forward or backward on the line. To flip through the book page-by-page, tap the arrows.

3.) Tap the page you are previewing to go to it.

If you'd like to return to the original location, tap the X on the preview pane.

Navigating with the *Go To* button

1.) Tap the top of the screen to display the toolbar.

2.) Tap the *Go To* button.

From there, you have various options: *Contents, Page and Location,* and *Notes.*

The *Contents* tab will display the book's table of contents, allowing you to navigate the book by tapping a chapter you'd like to go to. You can also select *Beginning* or *End.*

The *Page and Location* option can be used if you'd like to go to a specific page. Simply select the *Page and Location* option and use the onscreen keyboard to type in the exact page number. You can search by the page number or location.

The *Notes* section will display all of the text you have highlighted while you were reading. To highlight text, press and hold a finger on the onscreen words and use a constant swiping motion to highlight them. The *Yours* section will show you the text that you have highlighted, while the *Popular* section will display the text that was highlighted by other people.

How to Get More Out of Your Reading Experience

Digital reading devices certainly have their benefits, including the ability to adjust font size, immediately discover the meaning of a word, and more.

Dictionary, Vocabulary Builder, and Flashcards

To activate the dictionary while reading, press and hold the onscreen word you would like to find the meaning of. The word will become highlighted, and a moment or so later, the meaning of the word will appear on the screen automatically.

The words you have looked up will be stored in the *Vocabulary Builder*. To access the *Vocabulary Builder*, go to the menu and select it.

Inside the *Vocabulary Builder*, you can use the *Flashcards* tab to "master" words. Once you have memorized a word's meaning, you can mark that word as "mastered."

How to Customize The Text

1.) While reading, tap the top portion of the screen to reveal the toolbar.

2.) Tap the *Text* button.

3.) In the dialog box, adjust the font size, typeface, line spacing, or margins as you'd like them to appear on the *Kindle* screen.

Zoom in on Images

1.) Press and hold one finger on the image.

2.) Release the finger to bring up a magnifying-glass icon.

3.) Tap the icon.

Tap the image again to bring it back to its normal size. For select *Kindle* books, it is possible to zoom in further by placing two fingers close together on the center portion of the screen and moving them apart. If you'd like to zoom out, place two fingers spaced slightly apart on the screen and pinch them together. While zoomed, drag one finger across the image to move to an area of interest. Tap the X in the top right corner of the image to return to reading.

Searching within a book or document while reading

1.) Tap the top of the screen. This will make the toolbar appear.

2.) Tap the *Search* button.

3.) Enter the text you'd like to search for.

How to Bookmark a Page

1.) Tap the **Bookmark** button on the reading toolbar.

2.) Tap the *plus* sign next to the location or page information.

Bookmarks are added to the **My Clippings** file on the Home screen.

How to Delete a Bookmark

1.) Tap the **Bookmark** button on the reading toolbar.

2.) Locate the bookmark you'd like to delete in the list.

3.) Select (tap) the bookmark.

4.) Tap the X next to it.

Using the *Word Wise* feature

Word Wise can be enabled by tapping the menu and selecting *Word Wise*. This feature can help make it easier for readers to understand big words without having to look them up in an offline dictionary. Short and straight forward definitions will begin to appear above challenging words, so the user can continue reading without a great deal of interruption.

How to take screenshots

To take a screenshot, tap the bottom-left and top-right corners or the bottom-right and top-left corners of the screen simultaneously. The screen will flash, indicating the screenshot has been taken.

Note: The screenshots can only be accessed when the *Kindle* device is connected to your computer.

Connecting the *Kindle* device to a computer

The *Kindle* can be connected to a computer via the USB. When connected, *Kindle* will show up as an external storage drive or volume on the computer's screen. There should be a folder called "documents," in which *Kindle*-compatible files can be added, copied, moved to, or deleted.

Note: The *Kindle* device is not usable as a reading device while in USB drive mode.

Using the Web Browser

The *Kindle* devices has an experimental web browser that allows you to surf the web, though a WI-FI connection must be established to access most websites.

To launch it, go to the menu and select **Experimental Browser**.

To bookmark a web page, go to the menu and select **Bookmark this Page**.

Notes and Highlights

Notes and highlights can be added by pressing and holding the onscreen text and dragging a finger across the screen to highlight it.

To continue highlighting into the next page, drag one finger to the bottom-right corner of the screen. The page will turn automatically.

You can also "long press" (press and hold) a word to bring up another menu while you're reading a book. The menu will include various tabs, including **Highlight, Notes, Share,** and a **Search (magnifying-glass icon)** feature. Selecting **Note** will allow you to add a note to the highlighted text. In the options section (icon with three dots), you have the option to look up the word in the dictionary.

Time Left in Chapter

When you are reading a book, a *Time Left in Chapter* will be displayed at the bottom-left corner of the screen. You can shift through the various options by tapping the text. To illustrate, to switch from *Time Left in Chapter* to *Time Left in Book*, tap the *Time Left in Chapter* text. Continue to tap the text if you'd like to cycle through all the available display options.

How to Add Multiple Accounts

Adults and children can be added to the *Kindle*. Up to two adults and four children per household can be added. Two adults will be able to manage up to four child accounts, allowing the adults to control the content and features the children can access.

This makes it possible to share one *Kindle* with multiple people in your home without having to share the same library.

Family Library enables you to share digital content across your *Amazon* devices. *Family Library* can be activated when adding an adult to your household.

1.) Go to **Settings**.

2.) Select **Household & Family Library**

3.) Select the **Add a New Person** tab.

4.) Select **Add Adult** or **Add Child**.

5.) Follow the onscreen prompts.

Note: By choosing to enable sharing for an adult account, you are authorizing the second adult to use credit cards associated with your *Amazon* account to make purchases on the *Amazon* store.

Leaving a household will disallow both adults to start or join a household for 180 days. Additionally, the household will be disallowed to have another adult added for 180 days, and you will not be able to administer child accounts that are part of the household.

<u>Understanding Device and *Cloud* Storage</u>

 T he *Cloud* securely stores content that is purchased from the *Kindle* Store, including copies of all your books and recent issues of newspapers and magazines.

Cloud content can be accessed by tapping **Cloud** in the top-left corner of the Home screen or **All** in the top-left portion of the library screen.

Your documents are saved in the *Cloud* if they have been emailed to your *Kindle* and if you have enabled **Personal Document Archiving** in the **Manage Your Content and Devices** section.

If you'd like to view content that is stored on your *Kindle*, tap **On Device**.

Tip: If you plan to go offline and would still like to view content, tap **Cloud** and download any content to your *Kindle* that you'd like to have available.

Downloaded items can be opened from the Home screen or from the *Cloud*.

<u>How to Download Content that is Stored in the *Cloud*</u>

1.) Tap *Cloud* in the top-left corner of the Home screen.

2.) Tap on the items you'd like to download to your *Kindle*.

Tip: The download can be canceled by tapping on the item's title.

How to Manage your Content

The *Kindle* is capable of storing thousands of books, documents, newspapers, blogs, and magazines.

This list of content can be displayed by tapping the **Home** button, then selecting the **On Device** option.

View how much free space your *Kindle* has for storing content

1.) Tap the **Menu** button.

2.) Select **Settings**.

3.) On the **Settings** page, go to the menu and select **Device Info**.

Change the appearance of the *Home* screen

1.) Tap the **Menu** button.

2.) Select **List** or **Cover View**.

How to Sort your Content

By default, the content is sorted by Recent, which brings new items and the content you are currently reading to the top.

But there is a way to change the sort option.

1.) Make sure you are on the Home screen.

2.) Tap the name of the existing sort order, located under the toolbar.

Items that are stored in the *Cloud* can also be sorted.

Filter the content by type

1.) Go to the Home screen.

2.) Tap **All Items**, located under the toolbar.

How to Remove Items from *Kindle*

1.) Go to the Home screen.

2.) Press and hold the item's name or cover.

3.) Wait for the dialog box to pop up, then tap **Remove from Device**.

Note: This will not remove content from the *Cloud*. The content will securely remain in the *Cloud*, where it will be available to download at another time.

How to Transfer Content from an Old Kindle to your New One

Although most content is securely stored in the *Amazon Cloud*, there are certain documents that might need to be transferred manually.

Personal content that was transferred directly to your old *Kindle,* but was not emailed to it will need to undergo a different transfer procedure.

Download content to your new *Kindle* from the *Cloud* directly

1.) Go to the Home screen.

2.) Tap **My Library** in the top-left portion of the screen.

3.) You should now be at the library page. Tap **All** in the top-left portion of the screen.

Download personal content that was stored on your *Kindle*, but not emailed to it

1.) Using the USB cable, connect your *Kindle* device to a computer.

2.) Transfer the files or folders to the documents folder.

For more information about using the USB, refer to the *How to get more out of your reading experience* chapter and look under the *Connecting the Kindle device to a computer* section.

Cloud Collection

Cloud Collections allow you to organize the content on your device into customized categories that are stored in the Cloud.

The collections are synced between other devices that are registered to the same *Amazon* account and that support Cloud Collections. Items can be added to more than one collection.

How to Create a New Cloud Collection

1.) Go to the Home screen and tap the **Menu** button.

2.) Select **Create New Collection**.

3.) Using the keyboard, enter a name for the collection.

4.) Tap **OK**.

5.) There should now be a visible list of items that can be added to a collection.

6.) Tap the checkbox next to an item to add it to the collection.

7.) When you're finished, tap **Done**.

Add or Remove Items in a Cloud Collection

1.) Make sure you are in a collection.

2.) Tap the menu button.

3.) Select **Add/Remove Items**.

How to Filter the Content on the Home Screen by Collection

1.) Tap **All Items** or the currently selected filter.

2.) Select **Collections**.

The collections you download to your device will be displayed in the **All Items, Books, Periodicals,** and **Docs** sections.

If you'd like to download a collection, simply press and hold the onscreen collection cover or title and tap **Add to Device**. This setting is device-sensitive, however, and it will not be saved if you decide to remove your device from registration.

If you'd like to remove a collection, press and hold the onscreen collection cover or title and tap **Remove from Device**.

Tip: Deleting a collection from your *Kindle* will not remove the content stored on your device or in the *Cloud*. Items previously placed into the collection that are stored on your *Kindle* will still appear on the Home screen and in the *Cloud*.

Deleting a collection that was created on a device or in a reading app that supports *Cloud Collections* will delete it from the *Cloud* and other devices or reading apps that support *Cloud Collections* and are registered to the same *Amazon* account.

Periodicals

Magazines and newspapers are kept in folders that are grouped by periodical name.

To free up space on your device, issues that are more than eight issues old, newspapers that are more than fourteen issues old, and magazines that are more than forty issues old will be deleted automatically.

However, there are two ways to keep a copy of an issue on your device.

Option 1

1.) Go to the Home screen.

2.) Tap **On Device**.

3.) Press and hold the onscreen name or cover of the issue you'd like to keep.

4.) Select **Keep This Issue**.

Option 2

1.) Go to the issue.

2.) Tap the **Menu** (icon with 3 dots) button.

3.) Select **Keep This Issue**.

Maintenance

- When cleaning the screen, use a soft, nonabrasive cloth.

- When carrying the *Kindle* device in a suitcase, bag, briefcase, or backpack, keep a cover on it to avoid scratch marks.

- Try not to spill any food or beverages on the device.

- Keep the *Kindle* device and its accessories out of rain and away from sinks and other locations that can potentially cause water damage.

- If the device does get wet, unplug all cables, turn off the wireless feature, and allow the screen to revert to the screen saver. The wireless feature can be powered off by tapping the **Quick Actions** icon and enabling **Airplane Mode**. Wait for the device to dry entirely before waking it with the power button. Do not try to dry the device with a microwave, hair dryer, or any other external source of heat.

- Do not subject the device to high-heat or extreme cold conditions.

- Read all safety instructions for any third-party accessories before using them with the *Kindle* device. In some cases, use of third-party accessories may impact your device's performance and may even void the *Kindle* device's limited warranty.

- If the device requires service, contact *Amazon Customer Support*. Contact details can be found by visiting *Amazon's* **Device Support** page on their website. Improper service can void the warranty.

- The *Kindle* device's battery should only be repaired or replaced by qualified personnel.

How to Minimize Interference

If the radio or TV reception improves after powering off your *Kindle* device and grows worse when the *Kindle* is powered on, there are some steps you can take to minimize the interference.

- Reorient or relocate the receiving antenna for the radio or TV.

- Move the *Kindle* device further away from the radio or TV.

- Connect equipment and receivers to different outlets.

Safety

• To reduce the risk of experiencing discomfort, avoid prolonged use, hold the device a comfortable distance from your eyes, and use the device in a well-lit room.

• Stop using the device and consult a qualified physician if seizures, convulsions, or other discomfort is experienced.

• Small parts contained in the device and its accessories may pose a choking hazard to young children.

• Using the device while operating a vehicle is not recommended and may even be forbidden in certain areas. Stop using your device immediately if it becomes a distraction while driving.

• Pacemakers and other medical devices may be sensitive to the magnets and electromagnetic fields that the *Kindle* contains and emits. Such medical devices should be kept at least 15 cm from *Kindle* and certain accessories. If any interference is brought to your attention, consult a qualified physician before resuming use of the *Kindle* device.

• Hard drives, credit cards, and other items that contain magnetically-stored data may be sensitive to magnetic or electromagnetic fields, and shouldn't be kept near *Kindle* products.

• Power off the wireless connection in areas where wireless use is forbidden or when it might cause interference or pose a safety risk. Generally, you should not use the *Kindle* device with the wireless connection powered on anyplace where you are forbidden to use a mobile device, including airplanes, healthcare facilities, or construction sites.

• Most modern electronic equipment is shielded from from external RF (radio frequency signals. However, if in doubt, check with the manufacturer.

• If you are not sure if RF signals could constitute a hazard at the place you are at, look around for signs indicating that mobile devices or two-way radios should be powered off.

• If you are on a plane, ask a crew member when it's safe to power on wireless service.

• In certain areas, the disposal of certain electronic devices is regulated. Take care to dispose of or recycle the *Kindle* device in a way that conforms to the local laws and regulations.

Troubleshooting

Many issues, such as screen freezing, can be resolved by simply restarting the device.

How to restart the device

1.) Press and hold the power button for approximately seven seconds until the dialog box becomes displayed on the screen.

2.) Tap **Restart**.

If the device is so unresponsive that the dialog box does not appear, a forced restart is necessary. To perform a forced restart, press and hold the power button for approximately forty seconds until the device restarts.

Battery is not charging properly or is draining too rapidly

• Verify that you are using a compatible USB cable and that it is securely connected.

• If you are using a power adapter, verify that it is not faulty.

• Place the device into *Sleep* mode when you are finished reading.

• Power off the wireless connection to save power.

Can't connect to WI-FI

• Check the wireless connectivity on the *Kindle*.

• Verify that the wireless router is set to use a WI-FI channel from 1 to 11.

• Restart the modem or router by unplugging it and plugging it back in.

Can't remember pass-code

The device will need to be reset.

Important Note: Resetting the device will remove all of your personal information, including parental controls, your lock screen pass-code, *Amazon* account information, WI-FI settings, and downloaded content.

However, any content you have purchased from *Amazon* will remain securely stored in the *Cloud* and can be downloaded again after you register the *Kindle* to your account.

To reset the device:

1.) Bring up the onscreen keyboard by tapping the pass-code field.

2.) Type **111222777**, then tap **OK**.

You'll need to connect to a wireless network and register the device to use your *Kindle* again.

Content doesn't seem to download

- **Sync to receive the content**

1.) Go to the **Home** screen.

2.) Tap the **Menu** icon.

3.) Tap **Sync and Check for Items**.

- **Check wireless connection status**

1.) Go to the **Home** screen or any **Settings** screen.

- Make sure **Airplane** mode is not powered on.

- Verify that your device is running the latest software version.

- Verify that your payment method is valid.

- Check if you are filtering content on your Home screen. You can check by going to the Home page and selecting the **On Device** tab. Make sure it is displaying **All items**.

Content will not sync

- Check the wireless connection status.

- Make sure the device is running the latest software version.

- Verify that **WHISPERSYNC** for books is enabled on the *Kindle* device.

1.) Go to the Home screen.

2.) Tap the **Menu** icon.

3.) Go to **Settings**.

4.) Go to **Device Options**.

5.) Go to **Personalize Your *Kindle***

6.) Go to **Advanced Options**.

7.) Enable *WHISPERSYNC for Books* if it's not enabled already.

- Verify that **WHISPERSYNC Device Synchronization** is enabled on your *Amazon* account.

1.) Go to the *Amazon* web site from your computer.

2.) Go to the **Manage Your Content and Devices** section.

3.) Select **Settings**.

4.) Look under **Device Synchronization** and make sure that **WHISPERSYNC Device Synchronization** is on.

Book does not open

- Make sure that the device is connected to WI-FI.

• Remove the book, restart the device, and download the book again.